E.M.C.D.D.A.
European Monitoring Centre
for Drugs and Drug Addiction

Guidelines for the evaluation of outreach work

2

A manual for outreach practitioners

Information on the EMCDDA can be found on its website (http://www.emcdda.org).

A great deal of additional information on the European Union is available on the Internet.
It can be accessed through the Europa server (http://europa.eu.int).

Cataloguing data can be found at the end of this publication.

Luxembourg: Office for Official Publications of the European Communities, 2001

ISBN 92-9156-024-3

Printed in Belgium

To the memory of our friend and colleague Roger Lewis

9 March 1944 to 25 April 2000

'But he who kisses the joy as it flies lives in eternity's sunrise'

William Blake

Preface

●●

This is the second manual on evaluation in the EMCDDA's Manual series. It has a specific flavour, concentrating as it does on self-evaluation for outreach projects. It was intended from the beginning that providing a common language that fitted with the ethos of outreach work was paramount, whether it took place in railway stations or dance clubs, with young people or transsexuals.

The need for producing guidelines in this particular area was highlighted by an EMCDDA Insights report, *Outreach work among drug users in Europe*. It is hoped that these guidelines can continue the process of dialogue across countries and agencies about outreach and its development. The EMCDDA is promoting evaluation and highlighting best evaluation practice in order to improve the information available for decision-makers and practitioners.

Outreach work is an important means of accessing hard-to-reach populations. Traditionally, the most important target groups in the field of drugs have been marginalised youth (groups at risk) and the addict population. The HIV/AIDS epidemic has, for better or worse, strongly contributed to the further development, professionalisation and dissemination of outreach work among drug users.

Today, outreach work is also concerned with new trends in drug use. These trends include:

● new substances such as synthetic drugs;

● 'natural' or 'ecodrugs' (for example, psychedelic mushrooms, ephedra) with a long history but no widespread tradition of use and abuse in Europe;

● revivals of 'old' drugs, such as the recent increase in cocaine use in club scenes in several EU Member States;

● new patterns of use;

● and changing target groups (such as the homeless, asylum seekers and clubbers).

Consequently, these guidelines give examples from a range of outreach settings.

Developing these guidelines has been an iterative process. The writing was informed throughout by the general literature on evaluation and guidelines for other types of service. Outreach projects from across the EU were asked about their current evaluative activities by means of a questionnaire and this further shaped the document. A report explaining our thinking and containing draft guidelines was then discussed at a workshop in Lisbon, and the recommendations ensuing from that event helped to create the final version.

We would like to thank the following participants in the workshop:

Susanna Ronconni (Centro Studi Gruppo Abele, Italy), Anne Coppel (Association Clinique Liberté, France), Stéphane Leclercq (Energycontrol, Spain), Mathias Hofmann (Drogenberatung e.V. in Lippe, Germany), Dagmar Hedrich (Portugal) and Monica Dinis (Camara Municipal de Lisboa, Portugal). The team would also like to thank Gregor Burkhart and Margareta Nilson from the EMCDDA for recognising the need for these guidelines and responding so positively to them as they emerged. We are also grateful to Isabelle Houman for organising us in Lisbon and to Mags McMahon for her patience and attention to detail in Edinburgh.

Finally, the team would like to thank all their colleagues around Europe working in the outreach and evaluation fields who helped in the creation of these guidelines. We hope they prove to be of value.

Contents

Introduction   9

   ● Evaluation dialogue 1   10

Part 1 **Approaching evaluation**   15

Chapter 1   Why evaluate?   16

   ● What is evaluation?   17

Chapter 2   Four essential principles   19

Chapter 3   Outreach evaluation: our approach   21

Chapter 4   Empowerment evaluation   23

Chapter 5   Assumption-focused evaluation   25

   ● Understanding your assumptions   25

Part 2 **Designing and implementing your evaluation**   29

Chapter 6   Overview of the evaluation process   30

Chapter 7   Evaluation dialogue 2   32

Chapter 8   The four stages of evaluation   35

   ● Stage one: Why are you evaluating?   35
   ● Stage two: What do you want to evaluate?   38
   ● Stage three: How was the intervention planned
      and was this implemented?   48

contents

- Stage four: Did the intervention have the intended
  impact/outcome?   56

Part 3   Evaluation techniques   65

Chapter 9   Methods and data analysis   66

Chapter 10   Communicating and presenting your results   74

- Organisation of reporting   74
- Structuring the content of the report   75
- Report style guidelines   75

Part 4   Glossary   77

Bibliography   82

Introduction

Policy-makers and practitioners around the world acknowledge the importance of outreach work in the drug field, but the fact that it is a good idea does not mean that every project is of the same standard. Clients, policy-makers and project staff need ways of assessing whether projects are fulfilling their aims and objectives. This guide aims to help outreach projects:

- to understand their aims and objectives;
- to understand and value their activity;
- to improve that activity; and
- to show themselves and others their worth.

The format of the guidelines is, we hope, practical and useful. The guidelines are intended to help foster a vibrant evaluation tradition within outreach work that fits with other traditions within that field. This is not a textbook on research evaluation methods, because evaluation is more than simply circulating a set of questionnaires at the end of a project's life.

The main target audience for the guidelines is outreach project managers and staff. Our working theme has been *self-evaluation in consultation with stakeholders*. Briefly, we have defined self-evaluation as the process whereby individual projects assess and reflect on their performance. It includes the planning and implementation of action in the light of the assessment. It also includes the learning of new skills by project members. In Part 2, we expand on this perspective.

Stakeholders are individuals and groups who have an interest in the aims, objectives and performance of a project or intervention. This can potentially be a lot of people.

Although the focus here is on self-evaluation, we have not excluded the issue of external evaluation and, indeed, we hope that the guidelines will help projects to have a more productive relationship with an external evaluator.

Now, read on and eavesdrop on a rather familiar conversation...

Evaluation dialogue 1

Carla Buongiorno (CB) bumps into her old friend Roland Keinmal (RK) while attending a conference in Seville. They agree to meet the next day to catch up on what they are doing.

RK   It's good to see you again. A really nice surprise. Who are you working for now?

CB   A new organisation called Project X. It does outreach work in discos, clubs and bars. It's a completely different scene. What are you doing now? Are you still with the same drugs project?

RK   Yes, I am managing the streetwork project now. The main drug issue is heroin. But what I want to know is: why is everyone suddenly talking about evaluation? Am I supposed to guess what it is? Our funders want to know that we're evaluating what we're doing. I'm keen for our funding to be continued, but I'd also like to improve our practice, to know we're not wasting our time.

CB   Do you want to talk about it? I have a counselling qualification!

RK   Do you accept beer as payment?! Anyway, have you done anything evaluative recently?

CB   Well, it depends what you call 'evaluative'. We've got our day-to-day systems in place. As we are quite new, I think we need to write up how we got started and some of the lessons we've learned.

RK   Yes, we routinely collect data and frequently discuss what we are doing. I suppose I would quite like to turn that information into a document that I can wave under people's noses, even if only to prove how good we are.

CB   It's always a bit ambiguous doing a self-evaluation. I'd like to be objective and yet I know we're brilliant!

RK   What about your aims and objectives? Are they set by your funders or are they yours alone? And do they really reflect what you are trying to do?

CB   In the funding applications, we had to set out our aims and objectives. They might need a bit of reviewing in the light of our experiences so far, but they're not bad. And there is a national strategy that includes outreach, so we have to take account of that as well. Don't ask me what it says in detail though. I think it says 'outreach is a good way of contacting hard-to-reach populations', but it's not very specific.

RK   I think planners are well disposed towards outreach work in general. In my experience, funders think they want to see statistics, but when they just hear about the numbers of people seen, for instance, they realise it's not enough and then they start wanting to know what you are actually doing with those people. Unfortunately, this is usually rather late in the day.

CB   Oh, the evaluation person at the local authority has been quite helpful with suggesting things we could do. Sometimes an external person can add that extra bit of clarity. We've started to ask ourselves who is interested in our evaluation: clients, funders, workers, volunteers and management. Now we are trying to find out what each audience wants and to see if any of those needs overlap.

RK   Over the years, we've sometimes felt that no one is really interested, then suddenly everyone seems to want to know what we are doing. We've been exploring what we can say about our impact on clients. As a group we sat down and started to formally discuss how we are trying to affect our clients and their decisions. It was amazing how many things we came up with. You know yourself that one approach does not suit every situation. Some people don't want to know us at all, and ultimately that is their right. Obviously, there are many types of client, but they do tend to fall into general categories and within those categories there are various stages. I mean, everyone is an individual, but you soon notice patterns of behaviour occurring again and again. For example, there are the old-timers who are very sussed and mostly want equipment. Some want a chat and a few are concerned about the youngsters. The new users divide into those we might have a chance with if there were the back-up services to divert them into and those who look like they're heading for prison. It can be frustrating, because we can only work with what services there are in the area. Our effectiveness is always linked to the existence and performance of other services and also to central government policy.

CB   At least you have some services to refer people to! I'm really aware that so much of what we do is dependent on the context. We assume we can deliver our message to people while they are out enjoying themselves, but I don't know if that is actually very feasible. We are too new to look at impact — everything is still very developmental at the moment. However, we have a weekly meeting where we discuss what is going on, individual cases and any changes to the other services we use, things like that. We have a debrief after a major club/disco session. We're going to have a session where we look at six months of debriefs and compare them to our objectives. Are we really doing what we thought we would be doing when we started?

RK   It's interesting to think that, although we may not be able to say things have changed because we exist, if we weren't out there recording what's going on, nobody would have a clue what's happening. It's one of our 'unique selling points', as they say in business. There is an early warning function of your work and mine that should be invaluable to colleagues in other services, and to the policy-makers and funders. Recording that intelligence systematically is a standing item on our weekly agenda. We look at everything our people have heard and seen and decide what is worth exploring further and what might be useful to others working in the field.

CB   I agree. You have to play your strengths. We have tried to capture exemplar stories, things that we've helped sort out, or typical examples of the range of behaviours we are coming across. It adds a human dimension to the numbers of leaflets handed out and events attended.

RK I was told decision-makers don't often read the bit about how you came to your conclusions, unless they really disagree with what you are saying.

CB Well, I wouldn't spend nights worrying about causality and the nature of reality. That is what our clients are for.

This dialogue raises a number of issues that are dealt with in this manual. The chapters that follow will take you through the process of designing and implementing an evaluation plan. In Part 1 we discuss the nature of evaluation and introduce our approach and some of the key concepts that appear in the rest of the book. We advocate an empowerment approach to evaluation. We also argue that spending time understanding the assumptions behind what you do is essential for a useful evaluation.

Part 1

Approaching evaluation

Chapter 1

Why evaluate?

Evaluation is often associated with a demand to justify funding. However, we argue that outreach projects should have an evaluation programme not simply to justify funding but more importantly to maintain or improve the service offered by that project. Ultimately, drug outreach projects have been set up for a particular reason, often to reduce drug-related harm. It is in the interest of everyone concerned, particularly the target group, to ensure that the interventions targeted by that project are having the intended effect.

Outreach work is, by its nature, at the front line of drug services, dealing with people at a grassroots level. It must therefore be responsive and flexible in its approach. Because of the changing environment within which outreach workers deliver their interventions, it is clearly essential to keep up-to-date with 'how things are going'. With other types of intervention, it may be easier to get a clearer day-to-day picture of the work undertaken and the impact on the client group, simply because that kind of intervention may be less diverse and less flexible. There may also be an argument that outreach work has a higher turnover of staff and that, therefore, an ongoing and thorough evaluation process is essential to maintain the continuity of the service.

In summary, it is vital to incorporate evaluation mechanisms into the internal structures of outreach projects in order to ensure that the target group is benefiting from the intervention. The issues of funding justification, wider reputation and recognition will then naturally follow on from this.

What is evaluation?

In general terms, evaluation exists to provide an insight into how something is, compared to how it was planned to be. Evaluation should offer information on the value of any intervention that can be used to help alleviate the problems to which the intervention is relevant.

The key sense of the term 'evaluation' refers to the process of determining the merit, worth or value of something, or the product of that process.

We have considered these wide definitions with reference to outreach work and, based on information received from outreach projects across Europe, have identified that, for many projects, the purpose of evaluation sits on a continuum. Project staff either feel that an evaluation is a means of satisfying funders or they see it as a mechanism for improving their service. This is illustrated in Figure 1.

Figure 1. Continuum of the possible purposes of evaluation

Client- or community-led   Funding-led

Towards the left-hand arrow, evaluation 'is designed to help people help themselves and improve their programmes using a form of self-evaluation and reflection' (Fetterman et al., 1996). Outreach work is infused with an ethos of community development and empowerment, of coalitions between workers, drug users and their peers, often involving democratic decision-making processes.

Evaluation also has the power to justify decisions, particularly about funding, and this is important for all projects. Hence, the right-hand arrow ends at a point where evaluation focuses purely on the need to justify and secure funding. When this is the case, evaluation is likely to be focused exclusively on the concerns of funders.

It is important not to polarise these factors. We need to consider the influence of other factors on how we understand evaluation. Figure 2 offers our intended model and understanding of evaluation within outreach work. It shows evaluation as something which can have elements of a funder-led and empowering activity, as something which can both be conducted internally and externally, using qualitative and quantitative methods and aiming to offer information about process and outcome.

Figure 2. Model of evaluation within outreach work

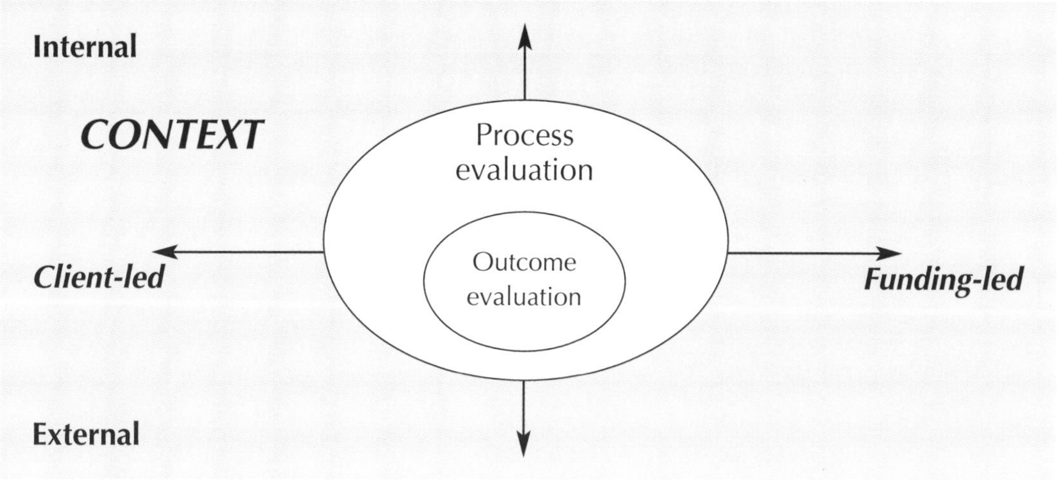

We have quite deliberately put 'outcome' within 'process', as the boundary between the two is blurred. Retaining an overly simplistic division between an outcome and a process evaluation does not really help in conducting an evaluation of aims and objectives that refer both to processes and outcomes. Finally, even if you decide to look at the impact of your service, you will have to start by seeing how that service was delivered. Thus, every evaluation starts with the process.

Chapter 2
∙∙∙
Four essential principles

In conducting an evaluation, it is important to bear in mind the following four basic principles which have wide acceptance in the evaluation community. Although they may seem obvious, it is very helpful to refer back to these points to ensure that the evaluation is on the right track. These four principles are:

▶ Utility

Perhaps one of the most important considerations which an evaluation should address is whose questions the evaluation is trying to answer. For example, what do stakeholders want to know and how should the results be communicated? An evaluation should be of use to someone!

▶ Feasibility

What resources do you have available to you in order to implement an evaluation? It is essential to conduct an evaluation which is realistic, so questions about available resources, timescales, budgets and priorities must be addressed and, once agreed, should be adhered to. It is better to have a thorough evaluation of one aspect of a project than to embark on a major evaluation of the whole project which cannot be effectively conducted due to lack of resources.

▶ Propriety

Consideration should also be given to issues of legality and ethics. Are the activities which you are planning for the evaluation ethical and legal? The evaluation process should never adversely affect those it is trying to help and all investigation must be conducted with regard to client confidentiality.

◉ Accuracy

Is the information you have collected accurate? Accuracy is vital to the overall worth and reliability of the evaluation. An issue to bear in mind here is selection of information. The evaluation may produce information which the audience would not wish to hear or that you are embarrassed about. We would suggest that, in these circumstances, you report honestly but highlight the fact that you are aware of the problem and offer a positive statement on how this may be resolved or tackled.

These four principles should infuse the design and implementation of all evaluations.

Chapter 3
Outreach evaluation: our approach

Over the years, different aspects of evaluation have been seen as more or less important. Countries have differing traditions. It has been observed that attitudes to evaluation have shifted from a preoccupation with precision to a focus on usefulness. Other trends include changes in the role of evaluator from distant observer to participant, and from academic to client.

These shifts are not universal and are still the subject of much debate. However, it is important that readers are aware of them because, for the purpose of these guidelines, we have taken one approach which we felt was appropriate for outreach work. Readers should be aware that there are many other approaches to evaluation and there is a huge amount of literature available concerning evaluation methodologies and philosophies.

It is also important to be aware that, although we have recommended one approach, this cannot be interpreted as a uniform evaluation plan/design across countries. The various cultural and social practices across countries do not allow such uniformity. The type of evaluation designed by means of our approach will depend on the state of the project (Has it only recently started? Has it existed for many years? Is the evaluation being undertaken to see if a potential intervention is needed or feasible?).

We have identified our main audience for the guidelines as being outreach project managers and staff, and our theme has been *self-evaluation in consultation with stakeholders*. We have defined self-evaluation as:

'the process through which individual projects assess and reflect on their performance. It includes the planning and implementation of action in the light of the assessment. It also includes the learning of new skills by project members.'

We have defined stakeholders as individuals and groups who have an interest in the aims, objectives and performance of a project or intervention.

There are four elements to the approach adopted in these guidelines:

- Firstly, in developing the idea of self-evaluation in consultation with stakeholders, the approach of *empowerment evaluation* appeared wholly consistent with the aims and objectives of much outreach work.
- Secondly, in considering the design of an evaluation, it seemed vital that an evaluation, particularly in terms of outcome, should try to understand the assumptions behind its activity.
- Thirdly, we discuss the concept of indicators. Indicators are pieces of data which act as surrogate markers and enable people to draw conclusions about a certain situation or event. For example, the number of people attending methadone programmes could be used as an indicator of how many people are using heroin. Clearly, indicators have to be designed to meet the needs of a particular project. This will be discussed in Part 3.
- Finally, the idea of outcome interdependence is crucial to these guidelines. A project's outcomes are affected, both positively and negatively, by the context within which they operate. This may refer to the impact of national government policy on the work and remit of a project or, on a more local level, it may refer to relationships with other organisations, such as the police or treatment agencies. Good long-term outcomes for clients depend on a network of services. The importance of appreciating the impact of context on outcomes is a theme which runs right through these guidelines.

Chapter 4
Empowerment evaluation

An 'empowerment evaluation' describes an evaluation which enables the stakeholders in a given project to develop appropriate and useful approaches to self-evaluation which will promote the development of the project rather than simply focusing on satisfying funders. Clearly, this fits in well with our suggested model for the evaluation of outreach work.

An empowering approach can take different forms and use many methodologies. It is not a blueprint for carrying out an evaluation but is a philosophical framework within which to design and implement an evaluation. In order to 'empower', the approach must be sustainable, so that project staff and volunteers can be taught how to conduct their own evaluation process. This also means that the evaluation process can be more internalised, which, Fetterman et al. argue, gives the staff power and control and demystifies evaluation. This sense of empowerment within the programme will help to break down fears and preconceptions about evaluation and will encourage staff and volunteers to use it as a developmental tool and not see it as an external threat.

Empowerment evaluation

- A philosphical framework;
- sustainable, so that project personnel can be taught how to conduct their own evaluation;
- gives project staff more power and control;
- demystifies evaluation;
- breaks down fears and preconceptions;
- a developmental tool, not an external threat;
- an outside evaluator is often brought in to give advice;

- a collaborative group activity, not an individual pursuit;
- an ongoing process of programme development;
- a means of self-determination;
- illuminating; and
- liberating.

Source: Fetterman et al.

Chapter 5
Assumption-focused evaluation

To work within this approach, it is vital that project staff and volunteers understand how the project was planned and implemented and what are the reasons for its existence — in other words, what assumptions the project is built on. Clearly no one can be empowered if they do not have this background information. Lessons cannot be learned and the project cannot be effectively improved if those involved do not have an understanding of what the project is trying to achieve.

An assumption is the belief that the implementation of a project will have a particular desired effect or impact. For example, a project may use peer educators in the belief that this will enhance the credibility of the messages they are trying to convey to the target audience. This may be a good assumption, but it is important to assess whether it is working in practice. A large number of such assumptions are common to many projects. Therefore, taking this approach will allow projects to compare themselves to each other, whether they use peer educators with drug-using prostitutes in train stations or with young people in clubs.

Understanding your assumptions

When any intervention is designed or discussed, there are usually a number of assumptions made by those proposing the activity as to why it is a good idea in the first place. These may be based on previous evidence of effectiveness or the professional experience and hunches of practitioners.

These assumptions relate to mechanisms that can influence individual choices. For example, a belief that information leaflets will reduce the transmission of HIV is an assumption. The mechanism describes how a leaflet could have this effect, so that it is possible to understand the reasoning behind the assumption. Continuing with the same example, people may pick, read and act on the information provided in leaflets on HIV because they are concerned about HIV transmission and want to minimise risky behaviours. However, these mechanisms are affected by contextual factors such as where we live, our age, health, education and a variety of other factors.

Mobile needle exchange example

This example will help to demonstrate exactly what we mean when we talk about mechanisms.

The aim of establishing a mobile needle exchange is that it will reduce the incidence of sharing equipment and therefore the transmission of HIV. There are many mechanisms that could contribute to people making a particular decision. These might include the following:

- Providing clean needles sends a message to injecting drug users (IDUs) that experts really consider clean equipment to be essential to their well-being, so they may choose to use the facility because they respect this expert/authoritative opinion.
- Use of the exchange facility may be driven by a general fear of infectious diseases, especially HIV or hepatitis.
- New needles are easier to use than older needles.
- Users may be concerned about personal hygiene.
- Users may derive a sense of ownership from having their own works.
- IDUs might enjoy a sense of authority when supplying/exchanging needles for others.
- A dislike of other needle exchange venues may encourage use of the facility.

These are all possible mechanisms that may have encouraged people to take up the offer of new equipment and therefore reduce their sharing. Identify what you think the key mechanisms are for your project and use them as a focus for the evaluation. For example, you may assume that IDUs will accept the offer of new equipment and advice because they are concerned about infectious diseases. In your evaluation, you should investigate if this is the case. Clearly, mechanisms are influenced by context and so will vary between and within countries.

These mechanisms need to be tested in an evaluation and this can go on to form the basis of a cumulative set of results that inform further practice (see Pawson and Tilley, 1997). This kind of approach can provide a common language and the chance to make comparisons between projects.

In summary, we feel that an approach that is driven by ideas about empowerment and the importance of assumptions and mechanisms is the most appropriate and useful theoretical framework for evaluating outreach work.

The next part will look at how these ideas can be pulled together to create a strong practical framework for evaluating outreach work.

Part 2

Designing and implementing your evaluation

Chapter 6
··
Overview of the evaluation process

The guidelines are divided into four stages. We will describe the importance of each stage in the overall evaluation process and indicate some of the key considerations to reflect upon. The flowchart (Figure 3) gives an overview of the total evaluation strategy. The potential benefits of conducting an evaluation are numerous, but it is important to appreciate that there are also pitfalls. While there are many textbooks on evaluation methods, there is a gap between textbook requirements and the actual practice of many evaluations.

In this part, we discuss a number of issues concerning outreach evaluation and provide practical guidelines for the design and implementation of future outreach evaluation. These guidelines are based on a process of consecutive decisions and in this way provide a decision-oriented model.

The guidelines are broken down into stages to present them as simply as possible, but many of the stages are in fact multi-dimensional. Your first self-evaluation should be a straight journey from A (the start) to B (the finish). However, you will discover that evaluation, like life, is not really like that.

Stage one: Why are you evaluating?

- Identify who needs or requested the evaluation?
- Agree the main audiences for the evaluation?

Stage two: What do you want to evaluate?

- Agree the aims and objectives of the project.

- Identify the interventions of the project, and the target groups and objectives they address.
- Agree the resources available for the evaluation.
- Decide which intervention(s) to evaluate.
- Define the specific aims of the evaluation.
- Discuss and identify how the interventions can achieve their objective.

Stage three: How was the intervention planned and was this implemented?

- Identify ways of collecting and analysing relevant information (include documents outlining the planning and implementation of the intervention).
- Match planned activity to actual delivery of the intervention(s) with commentary on issues that affected implementation.
- Identify and act on the lessons learned.

Stage four: Did the intervention have the intended impact/outcome?

- Identify how the intervention(s) can affect target groups.
- Identify the outcome(s) to be evaluated.
- Assess how much intervention the target group(s) received and whether this was likely to have the required effect.
- Consider whether the assumptions behind the intervention were justified and whether any changes are needed in assumptions and practice.

Chapter 7

· ·

Evaluation dialogue 2

A project manager, Roland Keinmal (RK), and an outreach worker, Donald MacDonald (DM), meet to discuss the project's planned evaluation.

DM   Hi, Roland. This is about the evaluation, right?

RK   Yes. When we discussed it at the team meeting last week it seemed obvious that everyone felt you were the person to coordinate it.

DM   Well, it's very flattering to be thought of so highly, but I'm not completely convinced. I mean, I'm a bit worried we don't have enough resources. We're all too busy to do any more writing!

RK   OK, but we all recognised why we need to do something. For one, the health authority, as our major funder, has been asking for something more than the monitoring reports we send them. But, just as importantly, I think we need to have an evaluation project to help us identify our strengths and weaknesses and improve our service.

DM   I know what you mean. There are lots of things we've discussed over the years that need looking at. I haven't seen those aims and objectives you circulated for quite a while, but I'm sure we could improve on them now.

RK   That would be a good place to start.

DM   But I do feel slightly aggrieved. People in the funding agencies sit in their air-conditioned offices having board meetings and free coffees and then they question whether they're getting value for money from a project they don't really give enough funding to. They've no idea what outreach work is all about and why it's so hard to record outcomes.

RK   So this is an ideal opportunity to help them understand. We could get some advice from an external consultant. If we work with her, the process will belong to us as much as anybody else and should help empower us.

DM   Wow! You've been reading those self-help books. Still, I get the impression that their hearts are in the right place. I think all the staff would find it useful to meet up with them and see where everyone's coming from. If this is going to work, everyone needs to have their say, and that includes the clients.

RK   Right then, I'll organise that. We'll have a team meeting — a brainstorming session — early next week. I'll bring in a spokesperson for the health authority, and we'll meet with all part-time and full-time workers.

DM   I think the big challenge is to make something of the data we have through our basic record-keeping. We see clients for such a brief time every session and we get as many details as we can from them and write them down back at the office, but this year's recording sheets aren't complete. Still, we're not trying to discover the meaning of life, are we?

RK   What was that you said about self-help books? So where do we start?

DM   It might be an idea to look at what we all do first. Get agreement on the key features of our practice.

RK   The funding body has mentioned to me that they would like to know what difference we're making to the lives of people on the street.

DM   You see! This is just what I mean about them being out of touch. Funders want to be able to say that outreach services are directly responsible for reducing HIV transmission in IV drug users and getting people off the streets. But it's not that simple. For one, it is hard to determine whether it is the actual outreach work that makes a difference to people's lives, because there are other factors at work. For another, we often make a real difference to people's lives and health, even if they stay on the streets. Sometimes just getting people a good shower once every three months is a really major achievement. Furthermore …

RK OK, hold it there. So you're telling me our project has different aims and objectives, some of which are easier to measure than others, and some of which are easier to achieve than others. We shouldn't be scared of evaluating, because it allows us to highlight all those issues. It is going to serve our purposes. So hold all those thoughts for the brainstorming session. We will follow that up with regular meetings over the six-month evaluation period, so you can share your ideas and complain and cajole and ask questions and get really involved. All we can do is help ourselves!

Chapter 8

•••

The four stages of evaluation

Stage one: Why are you evaluating?

- ⦿ Identify who needs or requested the evaluation.
- ⦿ Agree the main audiences for the evaluation.

The first question to ask before embarking on an evaluation is why your outreach project should be evaluated. It may be that you are at a stage when you feel that the project needs to be reassessed, perhaps because the client group is changing or you need to clarify or redefine your aims and objectives. In an ideal world, the best time to think about evaluating something is before you start. So, the following guidelines should help in planning for this.

In some instances, the impetus for an evaluation comes from within the project team itself, because staff and managers are interested in improving operations. It may be felt that the project is attaining its goals but there is no clear way of measuring the impact that has been made. In other cases, the evaluation is demanded by external funding bodies that are anxious to see that their financial contribution is making a difference.

Who needs or requested the evaluation?

The issue of who requests or initiates the evaluation is a very important one. It greatly influences the aims and objectives of the study, the questions asked and methods adopted. A funding body, for example, may require a report that gives greater detail on the distribution of funds and less information on the interaction of staff members or between staff members and management. Yet staff relations will be of great interest to a service provider.

Regardless of who initiates or conducts the evaluation, it must be designed to satisfy the agency's own purposes as well, which should be clearly defined at the outset. Thus, it may be that a funding body requests the evaluation in order to assess the project's financial requirements and future prospects. An evaluation should be devised that will address these issues to the satisfaction of funders while at the same time addressing the needs of project staff by identifying strengths and weaknesses and improving service delivery.

There is another matter to consider here. It is possible that staff within the project may be suspicious or fearful of an evaluation initiated by external bodies (particularly funding agencies) and this is also sometimes the case when the request comes from within the project. If not handled thoughtfully, it may be perceived as a threat or a reflection of lack of trust between funders and project staff. Thus it is a good idea to involve all staff members at an initial brainstorming session before the evaluation gets under way, as well as at follow-up team meetings. Staff members are important internal stakeholders. If all staff feel that their opinions are listened to and respected, they are more likely to participate fully in the process.

No doubt staff members and the management team, as well as other stakeholders involved, will have ideas of their own about strengths and weaknesses in the service delivery and how operations could be improved. It is useful for the aims and objectives of the evaluation to be articulated at the very beginning. Firstly, individuals are likely to feel strongly about the service and will be eager to have their opinions heard, so airing them early in the process will prevent any build-up of frustration. Secondly, all those participating in the process should be aware of preconceived ideas, so that the evaluation can be seen as transparent and not simply a means of proving the suspicions of various interest groups.

Figure 3. Map of possible stakeholders

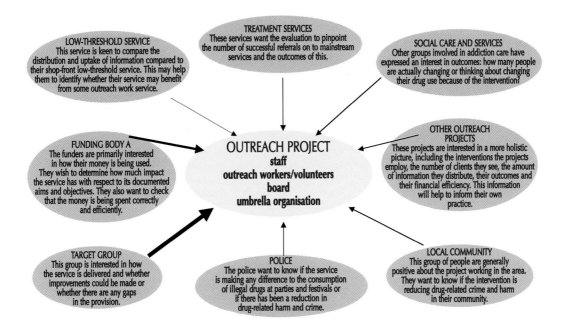

Who are the main audiences?

It is important to identify the main target audiences for the information from the evaluation. Obviously, these will include project staff themselves and funding bodies. Other groups likely to be affected are present and potential clients, other drug agencies, government and the wider community.

The issues that will be relevant for each group should be identified. Be aware how these groups may influence the aims and objectives of your evaluation. What will they want to learn from the evaluation? How can the evaluation help them to offer their contribution? Although it will not be possible to consult with all of the persons/groups who may be interested, it is a good idea to canvass a cross-section of stakeholders to gauge what aspects of the evaluation they are interested in and how they might want to become involved.

Exercise and example

In the first dialogue, Roland and Carla identified a number of stakeholders with an interest in their evaluation. To help identify stakeholders and their interests in the evaluation, we suggest that project staff (and volunteers) construct a stakeholder map similar to the one in Figure 3. This is vital, to ensure that all staff and volunteers have a clear idea of who the evaluation is for and what kind of information it will contain.

The stakeholder map (Figure 3) illustrates all the different groups of people who have an interest in the work of the project, along with their perspective on what they would like an evaluation to investigate. The varying arrow sizes illustrate the significance attached to the relationships between the project and different stakeholders. This in turn can highlight where the evaluation's main emphasis should be.

Stage two: What do you want to evaluate?

- Agree the aims and objectives of the project.
- Identify the interventions of the project, and the target groups and objectives they address.
- Agree the resources available for the evaluation.
- Decide which intervention(s) to evaluate.
- Define the specific aims of the evaluation.
- Discuss and identify how the interventions can achieve their objective.

Having agreed on who the evaluation is for, it is essential to establish exactly what parts of the project are to be evaluated. To do this there must be a clear understanding amongst all stakeholders of what the different parts of the project are and what they aim to achieve. This section will help project members identify and understand their activities in relation to their aims and objectives.

Agree the aims and objectives of the project

Before deciding on which outreach intervention(s) you want to evaluate, it is essential that you clearly articulate the aims and objectives of the project as a whole.

Aims should be understood to be a general statement about the end or ultimate goal of the intervention.

Objectives are more specific targets that will need to be met in order to achieve the wider aim.

Clarifying both aims and objectives at this stage serves two purposes. While it is extremely important to be aware of what the project is trying to achieve in the short and long term, it is also helpful for project and management staff to be reminded of specific aims and objectives, particularly to check if these have actually changed or evolved over time.

It is not uncommon for there to be some disagreement as to what are, or what should be, the aims and objectives of an outreach project. While some might consider that the aim of outreach work should be to refer clients on to other service providers, others may argue that the shortage of appropriate services means that the provision of *in situ* advice and assistance would be a more practical longer-term goal.

If disagreements arise between stakeholders, open discussion of these disagreements should try to bridge any differences. In this way, the evaluative process will have revealed differences that have probably been affecting the daily life of the project and that need resolution.

Exercise and example

Agree the aims and objectives of the project.

The overall aim of (your project) is: ....

....

To achieve this aim we have the following objectives:

1. ....
2. ....
(Add more as necessary).

It was relatively easy for staff at Carla's Project X to do this exercise, as they had quite a bit of documentation, especially from funding applications. However, the whole Project found it worthwhile to sit down and go through the aims and objectives, as it was not something they did routinely. They came up with the following:

The overall aim of Project X is:

▶ To reduce drug-related harm in the dance scene.

To achieve this aim, Project X has the following objectives:

1. To provide accurate, objective information about drugs and their effects;

2. to provide facilities to reduce drug-related harm; and

3. there could be others, many others.

Staff at Roland's project, Drugwatch, also identified their aims and objectives, which were recorded in their constitution.

The overall aim of the Drugwatch project is:

▶ To reduce drug-related harm and encourage IDUs to make contact with mainstream services.

The objectives set to achieve this are:

1. To provide facilities to reduce sharing of needles and consequent harm; and

2. To engage with IDUs who do not access services and act as a gateway to other services when requested.

Identify the interventions of the project, and the target groups and objectives they address

This is an important section, as it clarifies how interventions relate to the objectives of the project. It is very helpful to ensure that all stakeholders recognise the significance of each intervention to the wider goals of the project. In this way, the project is able to refocus, thereby increasing motivation among staff and volunteers.

Exercise and example

Draw up a table, like the one below for Project X, with the same headings. List everything your project does. Some things may naturally group together.

Table 1. Intervention and objectives of Project X

Intervention	Primary objective	Target group
Information stand	1	People who attend festivals/
Develop local information leaflets	1	clubs and who use or may be
Develop web site	1	thinking about using drugs
Chill-out facilities	2	
Crisis intervention	2	Users experiencing acute drug-related difficulties
Drug testing	1 + 2	
Training for club staff	1 + 2	Club staff

The four stages of evaluation

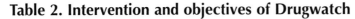

Table 2. Intervention and objectives of Drugwatch

Intervention	Primary objective	Target group
Mobile needle exchange	1	All IDUs
Information provision	1 + 2	All IDUs
Relationship building	2	IDUs who do not access mainstream services

Relate the interventions back to the objectives you agreed in the exercise in the section 'Agree the aims and objectives of the project' (p. 39). Try not to put every objective against each intervention. What is your target group for each intervention? Be as specific as possible and include settings as well. Use this list of interventions to decide what it is you want to evaluate (see the section 'Decide which intervention(s) to evaluate', p. 44).

Agree the resources available for the evaluation

This section is concerned with the feasibility of any proposed evaluation. How much time and money is potentially available?

Who will carry out the evaluation?

There are three options to consider when choosing an evaluator:

- hiring an external consultant;
- using a current staff member(s); or
- teaming a staff member with an external consultant brought in to assist.

Not all projects require an independent outside evaluator and, indeed, these guidelines are written specifically to assist project staff to evaluate their own interventions on a regular basis.

Nevertheless, there are times when it might be better to contract an outside person, someone with an objective viewpoint and evaluation experience. The main advantages to this are that he or she probably has access to more resources than internal evaluators and is likely to have considerably more valuable evaluation experience than an internal staff member. One further advantage is that external evaluators can offer a fresh perspective on the project that should be welcomed by staff. External consultants can be found at universities and other tertiary education institutions, state health departments or the private sector.

There are also potential disadvantages when bringing in an external evaluator. They may, for example, specialise in a kind of evaluation that is not very appropriate to your service. Since external consultants are not directly involved with the project, they are likely to have a limited understanding of the project's daily activities. They also cost money!

Another option is to allocate responsibility for coordinating the evaluation to one particular staff member or members. The advantages to this are that he or she should be very familiar with the project's aims and objectives and will have full access to all project activities. Furthermore, a staff member is likely to have more opportunities to gather informal feedback from other stakeholders. On the other hand, there are potential hazards in that it can be difficult for a staff member to be objective about the project's activities and outcomes. He/she may also lack the technical expertise required.

The third possibility involves teaming a current staff member with an outside consultant who will assist with specific stages of the evaluation (for example, designing questionnaires and/or data interpretation). It is important that the decision to employ a consultant is made at the start of the evaluation, so that he/she can be fully informed at all stages in the process. Do not wait until you are having problems.

Time and personnel planning

Another important organisational factor is the time scheduling of your evaluation. There are multiple factors determining how long should be spent on the evaluation. The most important consideration is whether there is any internal or external deadline imposed on when the results need to be available. Other considerations are the size of the programme, the resources that are available to fund it and the time that can reasonably be afforded, given staff availability and workload.

Many outreach workers complain about the difficulty of finding time to adequately collect and record data on their clients. Clearly, staff members cannot just have evaluation commitments tacked on to the end of their task lists. Time must be carved out of their schedule. If an internal staff member is in charge of the process, he or she must be allocated a timetable of hours that will be spent on the evaluation. If an external consultant is employed, the hours they are to spend will be quantified before they start. However, staff should also identify what hours they will be able to devote to participating in the evaluation.

Although the time-frame for the evaluation will be very different depending on the individual project, there are some commitments that are unavoidable.

- Based on the initial feedback, a structure for the evaluation should be drawn up by the evaluation coordinator within a set time after the brainstorming meeting.
- Regular meetings should be held between the evaluation coordinator and the project manager (if different). Depending on the timescale, follow-up consultations involving all project staff should be held at least once after the initial brainstorming. If the evaluation is to be carried out over a longer period, it may be wise to have such a meeting on a monthly basis.
- An overall time schedule is advisable, indicating the time-frame, the activities to be undertaken and the people responsible.

Decide which intervention(s) to evaluate

Often, when evaluation is at stake, the management, or those who have requested the evaluation, want to know everything about service delivery or interventions. However, limited resources will mean that the aims of the evaluation will need to be prioritised.

The more focus there is to an evaluation, the more efficient and effective it will be. In outreach practice it is often the case that one agency provides several services simultaneously. There might, for example, be a drop-in centre for drug users, a number of sessional outreach workers and a youth education programme. Alternatively, a long-standing regular service may be combined with shorter-term projects which are initiated when additional funding is available. Before beginning, identify clearly which part or parts of the project are to be evaluated.

It might be more cost-effective and efficient to evaluate the entire service at the one time. However, be aware that a more general evaluation may not allow for sufficient time to be devoted to each area of project activity. Limited time and resources may dictate that you prioritise which aspects of the evaluation are most important, so that at least some areas are covered comprehensively. The remaining areas can be covered briefly and left to be evaluated more fully at a later date.

Define the specific aims of the evaluation

After it has been decided what will be evaluated, it is important to clearly identify the aims and objectives of the evaluation. This will influence the type of evaluation chosen (see previous step) and will also relate to the stage the interventions have reached, ranging from exploring the potential for implementation to a well-established outreach intervention.

Example

Consider the example of Drugwatch.
Assume that the aims of the project are to reduce the incidence of HIV/AIDS and to improve the general health of the target population. The objectives are:

- ❍ to make contact with a large number of at-risk drug users;
- ❍ to identify their needs; and, where possible,
- ❍ to refer them to appropriate service providers.

Once these objectives have been established, the purpose of the evaluation can be identified:

- ● Is the intervention reaching its target population?
- ● Do the contact methods employed allow outreach workers to collect sufficient information on client needs?
- ● How many people are being referred to other services and what are the problems that have been experienced in doing so?

It is important to identify at the outset whether there is agreement between stakeholders as to what the aims and objectives of the evaluation should be. For example, if the evaluation has been commissioned by a funding body or the management body of the service of which the outreach project is a part, it may be that their focus will be different to that of the project staff themselves. This does not necessarily mean there will be a conflict, provided an evaluation strategy can be devised that will identify, and if necessary prioritise, the different objectives. Remember that an evaluation, whether internal or external, will only go well if it is informed by a clear and accurate idea of what is required. However, no evaluation can satisfy all demands.

Discuss and identify how the interventions can achieve their objective

It is very helpful to identify which elements of the project are to be evaluated and, using the previous table, to list the assumptions and theories behind each intervention (there will often be more than one). This is a good subject for a brainstorming session. The volume and breadth of discussion may be surprising and questions may also begin to emerge from the assumptions.

Example

Project X decided to evaluate its provision of chill-out facilities. This fulfilled part of their objective to provide facilities which would reduce drug-related harm. At the brainstorming session they came up with some of the assumptions they felt lay behind this work.

Intervention to be evaluated

Provision of chill-out facilities.

Objective addressed by intervention

To provide facilities which would reduce drug-related harm.

Assumptions

- People will rest/relax in this area.
- People will stop dancing and drink water.
- People will assess their current state of intoxication.
- People will engage with the information stand.
- People will enjoy the space and stay longer (longer rest = less harm from dancing?).

They now began to look at some of the underlying assumptions in more detail. For instance, if people are not staying very long in a chill-out space:

- Is it a problem?
- Is it right to assume that a longer stay means less harm?
- If so, is the space putting people off?
- Or is it being blocked up with people who do not want to dance at all?

Staff at Project X were beginning to experience the logic of evaluation!

Stage three: How was the intervention planned and was this implemented?

- ● Identify ways of collecting and analysing relevant information (include documents outlining the planning and implementation of the intervention).
- ● Match planned activity to actual delivery of the intervention(s) with commentary on issues that affected implementation.
- ● Identify and act on the lessons learned.

This section will encourage projects to consider what kind of information will be needed to fulfil the needs of the evaluation and what methods would be appropriate for collecting this information. It will also highlight the importance of acting on any gaps or areas in need of development uncovered by the evaluation.

Identify ways of collecting and analysing relevant information (include documents outlining the planning and implementation of the intervention)

It is beyond the scope of these guidelines to review all the existing methods of analysis that might be of use here, once the aims and objectives of the evaluation have been identified. However, there are some rules of thumb to consider when analysing data. Focusing on the link between evaluation and analysis helps to organise data and facilitate analysis. For example, if the main aim were a process-based evaluation to improve the provision of information about crack to at-risk youth in a deprived area, the analysis should be able to describe what, how and who contacted the target group and the (approximate) number of youths contacted.

The most effective way of making sense of the data collected is to use indicators. Indicators are quantifiable data elements, measured over time, that are used to track an intervention's use of resources and its performance. Such indicators can be quantitative or qualitative, as long as they are systematically recorded and fulfil the criteria below. For example, safer sexual behaviour is difficult to measure. The uptake by IDUs of free condoms given out by outreach workers on the street can function as a proxy indicator for safer sexual practices. The rate of uptake can therefore function as a measure, although it does not necessarily equal safer sexual behaviour.

It is very important to agree on what purpose a given indicator is to serve. Therefore, an indicator should be clearly defined:

- ❍ Can it be measured?
- ❍ Is it responsive to intervention inputs?
- ❍ Can it be estimated at regular intervals?

This last one is important, as it provides baseline data so that it can be monitored over time to see how effective services are and whether the target changes are being achieved.

When developing indicators, it is important to pay attention to their validity (does the indicator measure what it is supposed to measure?) and reliability (is it consistent over time?). It may be helpful to use the guidelines outlining the desirable features of a good indicator produced by the World Health Organisation (1994). Good indicators should:

- ❍ measure the phenomenon they are intended to measure (valid);
- ❍ produce the same results when used more than once to measure the same phenomenon (reliable);
- ❍ measure only the phenomenon they are intended to measure (specific);
- ❍ reflect changes in the state of the phenomenon under study (sensitive); and
- ❍ be measurable or quantifiable with developed and tested definitions and reference standards (operational).

Exercise and example

Identify the relevant documents outlining the planning and implementation of the intervention(s). These could include:

- ● the project's constitution;
- ● notes from 'away days' or similar events; or
- ● minutes from meetings discussing the aims and objectives of the project.

Project X has a business plan and minutes from an 'away day' that detail the aims and objectives of their interventions:

Aim

- ● To reduce drug-related harm.

Objectives

- ● To provide accurate and objective information about drugs;
- ● to build up good relationships with those people involved with the recreational drug scene; and
- ● to provide facilities that would reduce drug-related harm.

Project X was looking at the impact of their chill-out facility and decided to use a number of indicators, including:

- ● the number of people coming to the chill-out facility;
- ● the number of leaflets given out at the chill-out facility; and
- ● the number of requests from party organisers for a Project X chill-out facility.

See also Part 3, 'Evaluation techniques', for more on methods and analysis.

Table 3 offers further ideas about possible indicators and the type of information they require. These should help identify ways of collecting information or using existing information to answer questions about particular aspects of a project.

Table 3. Some indicators and the information they require

Indicator category	Data required	Example
If you want information about target groups, the following categories will be of use: ○ demographic ○ consumption ○ geographical/social	○ General demographic information (for example, age and sex). ○ Patterns of use (type of drug, frequency of use, quantity and route). ○ Geographical/social information (area of residence, employment status, education, marital status/children).	
If you need information about the type and capacity of an intervention and its progress, the following categories may be helpful: ○ aims/objectives ○ theoretical assumptions ○ needs assessment ○ number of 'activities' ○ client numbers ○ stakeholder opinions (including clients) ○ outcomes	○ Information about the aims and objectives of a project is fundamental. This is likely to be contained within an official constitution or perhaps in notes from an 'away day' or a mission statement. It will give direction to the intervention and indicate whom the intervention is designed for and what it aims to achieve. ○ If 'activity' is a needle exchange, collect data about the number of needles/syringes distributed and the number collected back in. ○ Client numbers should be broken down into relevant cate-	

Indicator category	Data required	Example
	gories according to target group (for example, number of clients broken down by pattern of use). This could also include data on number of new clients.	
	● Valuable information about the opinions of all stakeholders can be gleaned from a variety of sources. This provides very important data about how those involved in the project, either as staff, volunteers or clients, see the aims/objectives and the progress of the project.	
	● Monitor outcomes of intervention, by individual, and then compile to give a project-wide picture.	
For information about the internal organisation of the project, look at the following categories: ● accounts/financial information ● staff turnover ● staff and volunteer morale ● staff training	● Accounts and financial information will give a clear indication of efficiency and/or how the project is performing within its allocated budget. The production of this information is in itself an indication of how well financial records are kept. ● Data about the duration of employment may provide an important indication of people's experiences of working with the project. This can be attributed to a number of factors, including	Annual reports of other projects will demonstrate how they perform within their financial constraints.

Indicator category	Data required	Example
	pay scale, length of contract, intensity of work and external circumstances.	
	● Staff and volunteer morale may not be measured on a form but can be picked up in a number of ways: informal conversations, team meetings, staff appraisals, 'abnormal' attendance records, observation and formal feedback systems (that is, official complaints, etc.).	
	● Records of requested and completed staff training will identify outstanding gaps or issues for staff in terms of having the capacity to effectively carry out their duties within the project.	
For information on the background to the project/intervention, the following categories may be helpful: ● geographical ● cultural ● political (national and local)	These three elements will overlap, but can be roughly broken down as follows: ● Geographical indicators may include the unemployment rates of an area, population figures, local services (including schools and leisure facilities), crime figures, community relationships (for example, the police). ● Cultural information will tie in with the geographical element but will add information on the	

Indicator category	Data required	Example

different roles, expectations, interests and needs of these actors. Cultural indicators will also pay particular attention to the media. What is it about a certain group or area that creates certain unique patterns?

○ National/local policies (including drug policy, crime, social services, health, etc.) covering all aspects of life will feed into the experiences of drug users. How they are implemented locally will be of most interest to outreach projects. The national and local policies will affect provision of addiction care/harm-reduction services, provision of other support services (for example, assistance with housing), police intervention and drug education.

Monitoring and research aspects of the intervention:

○ development

○ Is the current system identifying new trends and new target groups? Is it acting as an early warning system? Are developments and changes within the project fuelled by information from the data collection and analysis systems? Are you reporting trends to other practitioners and policy-makers?

Match planned activity to actual delivery of the intervention(s) with commentary on issues that affected implementation

A first step for all evaluations is to describe what has occurred (that is, the process of the interventions): how much and what the intervention/project is doing. Volume and process indicators are used for this part of the evaluation. Volume indicators are data elements that describe the intervention's use (for example, the number of young people contacted during an intervention focused on the club scene and an overview of them according to age and gender).

Process indicators refer to what is delivered. For example, in the case of outreach work among polydrug users on the street, the focus would be on the content of the contact, how each session of outreach is organised, the number of referrals, the number of needles taken up, the content of conversations (safe drug use, health concerns and safe sex).

Most analyses include quantitative information. For example, an evaluation may have collected data on how many outreach workers are involved in a certain intervention, how many hours they have spent on the intervention and the percentage of streetwork activities in relation to desk labour. It may subsequently have collected data about the various activities related to both streetwork and desk time. This is important data on the process or implementation of the intervention.

Example

One of the targets Project X had outlined in their business plan was to:

● hand out 500 leaflets about the possible side-effects of ecstasy at their chill-out facility over a six-month period.

In fact they distributed only 100, because those using the facility wanted to engage more in face-to-face discussion and showed little interest in leaflets.

The four stages of evaluation

Identify and act on the lessons learned

This section is a reminder that, at the end of the evaluation, there will be lessons to act on. In the case of Project X, it became clear that there was more interest in face-to-face communication than in the leaflets they had produced. This is important information, but it is only useful if it is acted upon. Firstly, the project must recognise that there is a lesson to be learned; this relies on good data collection and analysis. Secondly, project staff and volunteers must be flexible enough to incorporate these lessons into their day-to-day work and to try to respond to the messages delivered in their data analysis.

There is no point in carrying out an evaluation or monitoring activity if the results are not going to be acted on.

Stage four: Did the intervention have the intended impact/outcome?

- Identify how the intervention(s) can affect target groups.
- Identify the outcome(s) to be evaluated.
- Assess how much intervention the target group(s) received and whether this was likely to have the required effect.
- Consider whether the assumptions behind the intervention were justified and whether any changes are needed in assumptions and practice.

What do projects find hard about evaluation? Often the main problem is demonstrating that an intervention actually made a difference. This is reflected in the excerpts below which were taken from questionnaires sent to projects across Europe asking about their outreach activities and evaluation procedures.

To evaluate the quality of the intervention and whether objectives relating to modification of behaviour have been reached (Italy).

Many contacts are brief interventions so it is difficult to measure effectiveness. It is hard to measure change in drug use over time as users dip in and out of services, and harder to specify that the service made a difference as a number of factors can affect drug use, for example, housing, relationship, general health, employment, etc. (United Kingdom).

To find the final results: when somebody disappears out of the streets we have no chance to know if we succeeded helping him/her or if he/she is in even bigger trouble (Finland).

There are no explicit criteria nor public demands for evaluation. Our main concern is to see if there are changes in the target groups we reach out for. We work with very operational/flexible aims and objectives which are highly influenced by the small number of personnel (France).

In only very few cases, it is possible to assess the impact of our intervention (whether behavioural change or health improvement (Germany).

We are aware of the need for evaluation. However, the often chaotic working practice, the lack of more or less standardised working procedures and data collection methods, make evaluation very difficult (the Netherlands).

Evaluating outcomes is clearly challenging, but it is also vital. This section will offer guidance on how to overcome some of the difficulties reflected in the above excerpts and confidently conduct an outcome evaluation.

Identify how the intervention(s) can affect target groups

This section refers back to the section 'Discuss and identify how the interventions can achieve their objective' (p. 46), which discussed what assumptions underlie interventions. It is important to consider the nature of the intervention and underlying assumptions and how these affect the target group.

For example, the Drugwatch project identified that their mobile needle exchange had been designed to target a group of people who do not currently engage with services and who inject drugs. Their assumption was that these people would use a needle exchange if it was not so geographically inconvenient, so they planned an intervention where the emphasis was on convenience.

One important concept to bear in mind is that of outcome interdependence. This is a short way of saying that the success of each individual project or service depends on the performance of a network of other services.

Identify the outcome(s) to be evaluated

In reality, it is often difficult to prove that an intervention has been the sole cause of a reduction in drug-related harm. There are too many other potential factors. Often it is easier to identify intermediate outcomes, which, it can be assumed, will feed into the wider aim. For example, if Drugwatch distribute and collect needles, then it is fair to assume that this will contribute to a possible reduction in HIV infection amongst that population.

It is a good idea to start by keeping things simple. Outcome indicators are measures to assess the impact of an outreach intervention on the target population. An example of an outcome indicator could be to discover how many of the referrals were taken up. Another potential outcome is client satisfaction; for example, clients' assessment of how well their needs are being met through indicators such as 'trust in the outreach worker'.

Assess how much intervention the target group(s) received and whether this was likely to have the required effect

This is where process evaluation is important. Only by describing what happened in detail can a judgement be made on what impact might be realistically expected. This section is best explained by using an example.

Example

A drug outreach project decides to measure the impact on the target population of information leaflets about ecstasy and testing facilities. Based on the results of a quantitative survey, they discover that the majority of the members of the target group do not test their pills at the facility. This project had been using the number of people attending the facility as an indicator of the success of the intervention and as an indicator for risky behaviour. They concluded from this survey, and using these indicators, that the intervention was not successful and that the target group was engaging in risky behaviour.

Further investigation based on interviews with the target group shed light on other ways used by the group to determine the quality of the pills — *a known and trusted dealer had already tested the pills.*

This example highlights the need to put data into context, particularly when dealing solely with quantitative data. Qualitative data is useful for this purpose and also to measure outcomes for outreach practice which cannot be defined or understood quantitatively.

When the data has been analysed, it will also need to be interpreted. This is a critical process, as the same analysis can lead to different conclusions. This is where the importance of placing the intervention within a broader social context comes to the fore. The following questions offer a guide on how to approach context:

- Do the results make sense? Do they make sense to the different stakeholders involved? For example, it may be that, despite an intervention which focuses on referral of HIV-positive IDUs to clinical treatment, a very large proportion is still not using combination therapy. Based on interviews with treatment providers, you may conclude that this could point to adherence difficulties among the target group. However, this conclusion may well be overruled when IDUs themselves explain that this behaviour is based on previous experiences of being excluded from treatment.
- What are some possible explanations for unexpected findings?

Consider whether the assumptions behind the intervention were justified and whether any changes are needed in assumptions and practice

It is important to revisit the assumptions the intervention is based on in light of the information presented by the evaluation. This is a key step in the guidelines, as it is from here that the service can develop to provide a better service.

Example

The Drugwatch project makes the assumption that a mobile needle exchange will 'work' because people will not have to travel into town to get clean needles. Despite a good initial response, further down the line the number of people using the exchange drops quite dramatically. Further investigation, based on informal interviews with clients at the fixed needle exchange, highlights that clients did not feel comfortable with a new member of staff who is running the exchange. The previous worker had been a former user who had also provided informal support and information.

So the assumption that people would use the facility for geographical reasons was not entirely accurate, as it was now clear that the person delivering the service was also a vital consideration. The information Drugwatch get from their evaluation will encourage them to reconsider this assumption, and therefore the design of the intervention which is based on it.

This is a vital step in the process. The aims and objectives of the project have been clarified and the assumptions which underlie it. Data has been collected to meet the needs of indicators which will help to provide information for the evaluation. Once this is all in place, it is essential to look at the resulting information and analysis with reference to the assumptions of the project. It is at this point that the evaluation is useful, but only if the information is acted on. If the evaluation indicates that an assumption is not correct, it is vital to ensure that this is discussed and necessary changes are implemented.

Table 4 goes through the process, from start to finish, of hypothetical evaluations for the Drugwatch project and for Project X.

Table 4. Hypothetical evaluations for the Drugwatch project and Project X

Drugwatch	Project X
The project staff identified a need for evaluation of their work.	The funders and management of Project X requested that an evaluation be conducted.
Aim To reduce drug-related harm and encourage IDUs to make contact with mainstream services.	**Aim** To reduce drug-related harm.
Objectives 1. To provide facilities to reduce sharing of needles and consequent harm. 2. To engage with IDUs who do not access services, and act as a gateway to other services when requested.	**Objectives** 1. To provide accurate, objective information about drugs and their effects. 2. To provide facilities to reduce drug-related harm.
Interventions A mobile needle exchange has been designed to target a group of people who do not currently engage with services and who inject drugs. (This intervention ties in with objectives 1 and 2.)	**Interventions** Various information resources have been developed to provide information to people who attend festivals/clubs and who use or may be thinking about using drugs. This ties in with objective 1. Crisis intervention has been developed to assist users experiencing acute drug-related difficulties. Training on drug-related issues is targeted at club staff. Both these interventions relate to objective 2. A chill-out facility is also run by the project and offers a space to relax and to find information.

The four stages of evaluation

Drugwatch	Project X
Assumptions about how and why these interventions might achieve their objectives include :	Assumptions about how and why these interventions might achieve their objectives include:

Drugwatch

Assumptions about how and why these interventions might achieve their objectives include :

- ◗ IDUs do not wish to share needles.
- ◗ Needle exchange facilities help to reduce the incidence of HIV/hepatitis.
- ◗ IDUs are less likely to use an exchange if it involves travelling.
- ◗ Bringing the service to IDUs will introduce them to services on their on terms and, therefore, be less intimidating.

Aim of evaluation

The evaluation is required to look at the overall impact of the mobile facility in reducing sharing of needles and in contacting the target population. The following indicators were developed:

- ◗ number of needles/syringes given out and number returned;
- ◗ number of clients and new clients seen;
- ◗ number of referrals to services apart from Drugwatch;
- ◗ number of referrals which result in an appointment being taken up; and
- ◗ qualitative data from clients about their sharing habits.

Project X

Assumptions about how and why these interventions might achieve their objectives include:

- ◗ People will engage with the information.
- ◗ People will rest in this area and rehydrate.
- ◗ The facility will give people an opportunity to assess their state of intoxication.
- ◗ Club staff will implement their training.

Aim of evaluation

It was decided to focus on the impact of the chill-out facility. The following indicators were developed:

- ◗ number of people coming to the chill-out facility;
- ◗ number of leaflets given out at the chill-out facility;
- ◗ number of requests from party organisers for a Project X chill-out facility; and
- ◗ qualitative data from organisers and people using the facility.

Drugwatch	Project X
Drugwatch selected several tools from the method table (p. 68) for collecting the data they required to inform their indicators. They opted to use stocktaking records, client contact sheets and observation.	Project X consulted the method table (p. 68) and opted to use stocktaking records, feedback forms, observation and diaries to collect the information they required for the indicators they had chosen to use.
After six months of collecting data to build up a picture for each indicator, Drugwatch produced a report. This simply looked at the results from each indicator and compared this information to their initial aims, objectives and assumptions.	After one year, Project X produced their evaluation report.

Drugwatch

Drugwatch selected several tools from the method table (p. 68) for collecting the data they required to inform their indicators. They opted to use stocktaking records, client contact sheets and observation.

After six months of collecting data to build up a picture for each indicator, Drugwatch produced a report. This simply looked at the results from each indicator and compared this information to their initial aims, objectives and assumptions.

Results

Their stocktaking records indicated that more needles and syringes were being distributed as time went on. However, the number of new clients was not increasing. Drugwatch felt that the rise in distribution was attributable to current clients becoming more used to the service. The client contact sheets recorded each new client and the number of needles they took and then brought back. It also recorded whether they requested any further information/help and if this resulted in a referral. If so, the referral was followed up to see if the client attended and this was recorded on the sheet.

The client contact sheets showed an increase of requests for information/help,

Project X

Project X consulted the method table (p. 68) and opted to use stocktaking records, feedback forms, observation and diaries to collect the information they required for the indicators they had chosen to use.

After one year, Project X produced their evaluation report.

Results

The data that they collected indicated that they had a steady number of people attending the facility at each event; they recognised that this was probably the most important factor for the funders. The uptake of leaflets had increased dramatically six months into the data collection. Stocktaking records indicated a 25 % rise in leaflets ordered. At this time, there was also a dramatic increase in numbers of requests from venues for chill-out facilities.

Information in the diary indicated that this rise may have been attributable to a recent scare in the press concerning the effects of ecstasy on brain functioning. Certainly the demand for information decreased over the following few months, but it was still high-

Drugwatch	Project X
and therefore referrals, but no increase in uptake of referrals. In conversation, clients indicated that their sharing had decreased since using the service. Drugwatch concluded that the mobile needle exchange was reducing the sharing of needles amongst IDUs. There was also an increase in referrals but not in uptakes. They are planning to redirect some resources to allow staff members time to accompany clients to their appointments. Drugwatch are also attempting to build up their client base by encouraging existing clients to tell acquaintances about the service or to pass on a leaflet with their details.	er than at the beginning of the monitoring. Through informal conversation and feedback forms, Project X was made aware of a demand to have more people from the project actually in attendance at the chill-out, rather than only the usual one person with leaflets. Project X concluded that the demand for their chill-out facility was increasing over time and that they should be more reactive to external influences such as the media attention to ecstasy. They intend, on the basis of their findings, to have two people at their chill-out facility (1 member of staff, 1 volunteer) to provide more of a 'face' for the project. These changes will be monitored in the same way and reassessed on a six-monthly basis.

Part 3

Evaluation techniques

Chapter 9

Methods and data analysis

This part will discuss how the information necessary for an evaluation can be collected and analysed. This information is often referred to as data. Many people think that the term 'data' refers to numerical information only, but it can also be used for things such as facts, statistics and observations. In order to depict the differences between types of data, and the methods used to collect this data, the terms 'quantitative' and 'qualitative' are used. Rather than understanding qualitative and quantitative approaches as polar opposites, it is useful to consider the data and methods as being placed on a qualitative/quantitative continuum.

Very simply, *qualitative* methods collect data that will show the situation through the eyes of those involved. The qualitative approach aims to observe and understand events within a context, paying particular attention to the complexity of the interactions which result in an event or situation. Qualitative approaches tend to favour methods such as participant observation and interviewing to uncover the more holistic and complex network of interactions which work together to create situations.

Quantitative methods aim to collect data that can describe and represent events, concepts, situations, etc., using numbers. This type of data tends to be used to highlight trends and patterns and is also helpful for comparative purposes.

Qualitative data are very useful for the evaluation of outreach projects. The nature of outreach work means that, although quantitative data is important, it must be put in context. For example, a streetwork project may have 50 contacts in one week and 25 referrals, but this data says nothing about the type of contact, the outcome of the interventions, the level of success with individuals with complex needs and so on. The numbers are meaningful only if augmented with other information. So, referring back to the idea of a qualitative/quantitative continuum, a solution may be to develop an approach which is a balanced mix of both methods.

The key is to select methods that match needs as opposed to, for example, perceived scientific credibility or ideas from important stakeholders. Outreach projects are often faced with evaluation requirements from external agencies which have a strong focus on quantitative data production. This may be a genuine requirement but is also often related to the widespread belief that quantitative data are 'real' and a consequent lack of understanding about the richness and usefulness of qualitative data. Over the last decade, this view has mellowed, possibly in part due to the shift in official health department attitudes away from the traditional medical model to a more socially oriented approach embracing qualitative thinking.

When selecting methods of data collection, it is important always to bear in mind the aims and objectives of the evaluation. This should be the driving force behind the decisions on methodology. It may sound trivial, but practice shows that it is easy to lose sight of the aims and objectives of the evaluation when the issue of methods is under discussion. A second important point in this decision-making process is the incorporation of cost and feasibility into the discussion, as certain methods are more expensive and/or require more specific expertise in using them. Methods must be chosen which are within the available resources.

As a rule of thumb, it is useful to begin by listing the existing data held by the project which may be suitable for the evaluation. Based on this overview, it can subsequently be decided if any additional data collection is required and, if so, what methods would be most appropriate.

It is important to realise that all methods will have strengths and weaknesses and that no single method can provide all the information required. Therefore, it is recommended that several methods be used simultaneously. However, it may be better, initially, to apply a few methods in a good way rather than many methods in a bad way!

Clearly, the methods chosen will depend on each individual evaluation. Table 5 gives an overview of a variety of data collection methods, structured according to the actual practice of outreach projects in Europe. It begins with data collection methods which are often already in place and subsequently mentions some additional methods for consideration. According to the information received from outreach projects operating in Europe, it is apparent that quantitative data collection is the most widely used. The method of collection is generally client contact forms, which collect data about numbers of interventions, type of interventions and (limited) client details.

Although methods for collecting qualitative data do exist, particularly in the form of diaries recording detailed descriptions of interventions, it can be difficult to extract the information from these and present it in a meaningful and reliable way. Many projects have little time to collect and reflect upon qualitative data, even when they believe this would be extremely useful. One project coordinator working for a long-established outreach project told us that their database allows only for the collection of limited quantitative data such as who is seen and when and the type of contact made. In his words, 'It's bean-counting really'. In such instances, any assessment of how the project is actually working can only be described as 'guesswork'.

A combination of methods collecting both qualitative and quantitative data, selected according to the needs of the evaluation, is the most useful approach.

Table 5. Methods which can be used for data collection

Method	Purpose	Advantages	Challenges
Client contact sheets	Standardised recording of clients' details and socio-demographic characteristics, often in combination with type of intervention (for example, contact or referral), mainly for aggregated quantitative purposes.	Easy to administer. Easy to analyse. Can hint at client progress.	Does not give any information about context. Is not suitable for all types of work.

Method	Purpose	Advantages	Challenges
Computer-based data collection	For recording general information (usually quantitative) about clients' characteristics and type of intervention; often based on client contact sheets.	Makes analysing and manipulating data quick and easy.	Requires trained personnel. Requires suitable hard- and software. Requires maintenance.
Feedback forms for clients	'Snapshot' information about client views and impact of intervention.	Allows clients to give feedback anonymously. Quick and easy to administer.	Possible low return rate. Difficult to follow up individual issues, especially if anonymous (question of utility). Assumes literacy.
Case notes	Information on pre-selected individual aspects of clients (mostly qualitative/ non-standardised information).	Provides individualised information on clients' characteristics and relevant contextual information.	Aggregation of individual information.
Log books/diaries	Provision of in-depth information on individual clients and observations about changes in target groups, often used in an informal way for team meetings.	In-depth and contextual information.	Can be time-consuming and requires commitment from all staff. Less easy to analyse and aggregate.

Method	Purpose	Advantages	Challenges
Minutes of internal group meetings.	Accountability.	Provides information on process development, issues at stake and agreements made.	Requires people to take the minutes regularly.
Stocktaking records (for example, for needles or condoms provided, publication materials distributed).	For indicators of output.	Provides insight into output and can function as part of outcome measurement. Can give an indication of patterns and trends. Functions also as audit requirements.	Cannot function directly as outcome indicator.
Auditing of financial records and accounts.	For information about efficiency and cost effectiveness.	● good practice anyway; ● vital to ensure money is properly spent and accounted for.	Does not indicate impact or quality of service.
Analysis of existing documentation: Internal (annual reports, publicity about project). External (other projects and stakeholders of importance).	Selection of information which is potentially suitable for the evaluation purpose.	Uses existing resources to highlight value. Useful contextual information to complement other data. Avoids reinventing the wheel.	Could be difficult to collate and analyse. Can be time-consuming. Data restricted to what already exists.

Method	Purpose	Advantages	Challenges
Scientific and grey literature.		Relatively little interruption of project's activities.	
Surveys.	To obtain information for evaluation purposes from a sample of the target population.	Information can be provided anonymously. Can be administered to many people. Relatively easy to analyse.	Depending on the type of survey, survey experts need to be hired.
Face-to-face interviews with clients.	To gather more detailed information about the impact of the service from the client's perspective or unmet client needs.	Possible to gather in-depth information about the impact of the service. Can strengthen worker–client interaction	Time-consuming and costly. Requires trained interviewers. Interviewer can bias client's responses. Depending on topic under investigation, access to target group can be difficult (for example, HIV/AIDS).
Face-to-face interviews with staff.	To obtain process information about internal management and working practices.	Can gather in-depth information not captured by already documented information.	Requires trained interviewer. May create tensions.

Method	Purpose	Advantages	Challenges
Face-to-face interviews with other stakeholders.	For detailed information about the relationships the service has within the wider network and perceptions of stakeholders about the project.	Provides a useful perspective on how the service is perceived externally.	Can be time-consuming. May need external consultant (expensive). May create/exacerbate tensions.
Focus group.	To explore the relevant issues among stakeholders (clients, other agencies, etc.), either among one group of stakeholders or a mixture.	Can be an efficient way to obtain much range and depth of information in a short time.	Needs a good facilitator. Scheduling may be difficult.
Ethnographic. Observation/participation.	To gather insight into how the project/ intervention/ target group operates.	Gathers information from the inside-out and bottom-up.	Requires trained workers, in order to interpret what is seen. Access.
Case studies.			Time-consuming and expensive. Can influence behaviour of those concerned.

Method	Purpose	Advantages	Challenges
	Provides in-depth understanding of a target group of clients, highlighting similarities and differences.	Provides information about clients' experiences of the intervention. Enables comparison. If presented positively, can enhance the image of the intervention to outsiders.	Time-consuming. Provides more depth than breadth.

Chapter 10
· ·
Communicating and presenting your results

In this section, guidance is offered about the communication and presentation of eval-uation results. Disseminating evaluation results to internal and external stakeholders and other interested parties can fulfil many objectives. These may include demon-strating the project's relevance, improving working practice, accounting to funding and regulatory bodies, informing local communities and gaining support for current and future projects.

Above all, the presentation of the evaluation should always be linked to the initial aims and objectives of the project, as well as to the target audiences. There are a vari-ety of approaches and tools for presenting results, of which the written report is the most well known. We will, therefore, focus on the presentation of results in a written report format. However, it might also be useful to consider other forms of presenta-tion, such as oral presentations, press releases and media communication.

Independent of the target audience, any report should be presented in an appropriate and attractive manner, as this will increase its chance of being read and understood. This is especially important if it is to be the basis for making decisions. It may sound like a cliché, but it is quality and not quantity that counts. Readers can lose concen-tration when a report is too long and policy-makers and others may simply not have time to read through a very thick report (even when it is excellent).

Organisation of reporting

Remember, the writing process should start before the actual writing! The writing-up of the results is part of the overall evaluation process and should be reflected upon from the start. It may sound obvious, but reporting requires a well thought-out plan-ning procedure. First of all, projects often have to meet a deadline with their written results. Apart from issues relating to editing and reproduction, it is also advisable to discuss and review draft versions with internal and external stakeholders, so that useful feedback or potential problems can be acted on at an early stage.

Structuring the content of the report

The information to be included in the report is dependent on the target audience(s) and what they need to know or are interested in. Depending on the target audience, the level and scope of content can vary even when addressing the same issues. The following checklist can help in ensuring that the most relevant issues are addressed in the report.

- ❍ Include an introduction outlining the background of the outreach project and the objectives of the intervention(s) evaluated, including work procedures and target group characteristics. The objectives of the evaluation should also be clearly set out. If the evaluation is a follow-up, describe any changes since the last report.
- ❍ Mention who commissioned and who conducted the evaluation.
- ❍ Describe how the evaluation was conducted, what methods were employed and in what time-frame.
- ❍ Provide the results and an analysis of the evaluation, and the framework which was used to interpret the findings, as this enables readers to understand how you have reached your conclusions.
- ❍ Present a summary of the findings and recommendations. If possible, describe what future actions will be undertaken or what issues need to be resolved.
- ❍ Policy-makers and funders appreciate the inclusion of an executive summary (that is, a summary of conclusions and recommendations).
- ❍ In the appendices, you should include relevant information about working procedures (for example, questionnaires, interview guides) or more detailed information about the data (for example, tables).

Report style guidelines

The report should have a clear title referring to the evaluation, and include the date and the names of the authors. We have come across many interesting reports which lack this basic type of information, making any follow-up or listing of references unnecessarily complicated.

It is helpful to structure the report with sections which reflect the issues discussed in the previous section. Each section should start with an interesting heading and include the appropriate information, providing clarity and making the information more interesting. The readability of the report should be a priority, so avoid unnecessary professional jargon and keep sentences short.

The written text can be illustrated by various graphic displays such as charts, graphs and tables. The type of visual tools you choose will depend on the audience and the information being presented. The text can also be illustrated by more personal stories, which often bring the data to life. These can be put in boxes, for example, or can have a different layout from the overall text.

If time and resources allow, it is a good idea to get someone else to edit and check the final report. If not, do try to leave several days between the writing and the final editing, as this allows for a fresh appraisal.

Ensure that the final report is distributed to the audience in good time. Consider organising a small launch event or something similar in order to encourage people to read and discuss the report. This will add to the impact of the paper.

Good presentation of the findings of the evaluation is vital to ensure that the report is read, understood and acted on where necessary. By following these points on presentation, the impact and utility of the evaluation can be maximised.

Part 4

Glossary

Aim

An aim is a general statement about the end or ultimate goal of the intervention.

Assumptions

This refers to the thinking behind an intervention and why it was thought it would achieve a certain outcome.

Assumption-focused evaluation

This approach to evaluation emphasises the need to understand the origins of the project in terms of the ideas and beliefs it is based on. This approach requires projects to understand and break down these assumptions, which are then analysed in order to inform the evaluation.

Empowerment evaluation

This kind of evaluation is designed to enable stakeholders of projects/programmes to develop appropriate approaches to self-evaluation which will promote the development of the project.

Evaluation

This is the process of determining the merit, worth or value of something to the product of that process. Evaluation exists to provide an insight into how something is, compared to how it should be.

External evaluation

This is primarily conducted and/or organised by people who are not connected with the project.

Indicators

These are quantifiable data elements, measured over time, that are used to track an intervention's use of resources and performance.

Input/output evaluation

This measures how much and what the intervention is doing. It is also known as a process evaluation.

Instruments

Instruments refer to all the methods used to collect information on the target group, the evaluation and so on. The most widely used instruments in evaluation are self-report questionnaires, tests, ratings and observation instruments.

Intervention

This is an activity designed to produce a certain outcome in a target group.

Interview

In evaluation research, interviews are used to assess data on the implementation process and outcome. Interviews can differ in their degree of standardisation (whether structured, semi-structured or unstructured), the type of contact (face-to-face, telephone or written) or the number of people interviewed at the same time (individuals or groups).

Mechanism

This refers to the relationship or link that exists between an intervention and the context it operates in to produce a certain outcome.

Objective

Objectives are more specific targets that will need to be met in order to achieve the wider aim.

Objectivity

Objectivity is, along with reliability and validity, an important indicator for the quality of an instrument. It refers to the fact that the results yielded by the instrument are independent of the person measuring the data; different people using the same instrument should achieve the same results.

Outcome evaluation

This kind of evaluation looks at the consequences of the intervention for the target group.

Outreach work

A means of contacting a target group on its own territory. For the purposes of these guidelines, we are targeting detached outreach work (that is, work on the streets).

Peer

From 'peer group'. This is a trained volunteer who belongs/belonged to the target population (drug user, prostitute, etc.). They are usually involved in peer support or peer education projects.

Planning evaluation

This is an evaluation aimed at exploring the potential for an intervention to be introduced.

Process evaluation

A process evaluation measures how much and what the intervention is doing.

Qualitative methods

Qualitative approaches to evaluation aim to understand a programme, or particular aspects of it, as a whole. Instead of entering the study with a pre-existing set of expectations for examining or measuring processes and outcomes (quantitative approach), the emphasis is on detailed description and in-depth understanding as it emerges from direct contact and experience with the programme and its participants. Qualitative data rely on observation, interviews, case studies and other means of fieldwork. This approach can be appropriate alone or in combination with quantitative approaches; for example, when a programme emphasises individualised outcomes, when there is concern for programme quality, or when the goals of a programme are rather vague. Qualitative data cannot easily be summarised in numerical terms, but they may be transformed into quantitative data.

Quantitative methods

Quantitative data are observations that can easily be represented numerically, such as answers to structured questionnaires. Quantitative approaches to evaluation are concerned primarily with measuring a finite number of specified outcomes. The emphasis is on measuring, summarising, aggregating and comparing measurements and on deriving meaning from quantitative analyses. Techniques often used in quantitative approaches are experimental designs and employment of control groups.

Questionnaire

A questionnaire is a list of questions, the answers to which can be systematically assessed. Depending on the answering mode, questionnaires may have open answers (where the respondents have to formulate the answers themselves) or closed answers (where they have to choose between several possible answers).

Self-evaluation

This is the process through which individual projects assess and reflect on their performance. It includes the planning and implementation of action in the light of the assessment. It also includes the learning of new skills by project members.

Stakeholders

Stakeholders are individuals and groups who have an interest in the aims, objectives and performance of a project or intervention. This can potentially be a lot of people.

Target group

This is the population for which the intervention is designed.

Bibliography

Aldrich, M. R. (1990), 'Creating a profession: Training outreach workers for AIDS intervention among drug users', in A. S. Trebach and K. B. Zeese, *The great issues of drug policy*, The Drug Policy Foundation, Washington, DC.

Bryman, A. and Burgess, G. (1999), *Analysing qualitative data*, Routledge, London.

European Monitoring Centre for Drugs and Drug Addiction (1997), *Evaluating drug prevention in the European Union*, Scientific Monograph Series 1, EMCDDA, Lisbon.

European Monitoring Centre for Drugs and Drug Addiction (1998), *Evaluating drug prevention in the European Union*, Scientific Monograph Series 2, EMCDDA, Lisbon.

European Monitoring Centre for Drugs and Drug Addiction (1999), *Evaluating the treatment of drug abuse in the European Union*, Scientific Monograph Series 3, EMCDDA, Lisbon.

Fetterman, D. M., Kaftarian, S. J. and Wandersman, A. (1996), *Empowerment evaluation: Knowledge and tools for self-assessment and accountability*, Sage Publications, London.

Fountain, J. (1999), *Profile of qualitative research on demand reduction: UK* (http://www.qed.org.uk/profiles/uk).

Frechtling, J. and Sharp-Westat, L. (eds) (1997), *User-friendly handbook for mixed-method evaluations*, National Science Foundation/Directorate for Education and Human Resources, Arlington.

Grant, I. (1997), *An evaluation of outreach work in Lothian*, CHADS, Edinburgh.

Klose, A. and Steffan, W. (1997), *Streetwork und mobile Jugendarbeit in Europa*, Europäische Streetwork-Explorationsstudie, Münster, Votum Verl.

Korf, D., Riper, H., Freeman, M., Lewis, R., Grant, I., Jacob, E., Mougin, C. and Nilson, M. (eds) (1999), *Outreach work among drug users in Europe: Concepts, practice and terminology*, Insights Series Number 2, EMCDDA, Lisbon.

Lewis, R. and Sherval, J. (1997), *New synthetic drugs: Demand reduction activities in the European Union*, CHADS, Edinburgh.

Needle, P. et al. (1998), 'HIV prevention with drug-using populations: Current status and future prospects', *Public Health Reports*,113, Suppl 1, pp. 4–18.

McNamara, C. *Basic guide to program evaluation*, Free Management Library (http://www.mapnp.org/library).

Miles, M. B. and Huberman, A. M. (1994), *Qualitative data analysis: An expanded sourcebook*, Sage Publications, London.

Patton, M. Q. (1997), *Utilization-focused evaluation: The new century text*, Sage Publications, London.

Pawson, R. and Tilley, N. (1997), *Realistic evaluation*, Sage Publications, London.

Rhodes, T. (1993), 'Time for community change: What has outreach to offer?', *Addiction*, 88, pp. 1317–1320.

Rhodes, T. (1996), *Outreach work with drug users: Principles and practice*, Council of Europe Publishing.

Rossi, P. and Freeman, H. (1993) *Evaluation: A systematic approach*, Sage Publications, London.

Shadish, W. (1994), 'Need-based evaluation theory: What do you need to know to do good evaluation?', *Evaluation Practice*, 15, pp. 347–358.

Shadish, W. (1998), 'Presidential address: Evaluation theory is who we are', *American Journal of Evaluation*, 19, pp. 1–19.

Shadish, W., Cook, T. D. and Leviton, L. C. (1991), *Foundations of program evaluation: Theories of practice*, Sage Publications, London.

Stel, J. V. D. (ed.) (1998), *Handbook prevention: Alcohol, drugs and tobacco*, Dutch Ministry of Public Health, Welfare and Sport, Amsterdam.

Van der Eyken, W. (1992), *Introducing evaluation*, Bernard van Leer Foundation, The Hague.

W. K. Kellogg Foundation (1998), *Evaluation handbook* (http://www.wkkf.org/Publications/eval-hdbk/default.htm).

World Health Organisation (1994), *Indicators to monitor maternal health goals*, World Health Organisation, Geneva.

European Monitoring Centre for Drugs and Drug Addiction

Guidelines for the evaluation of outreach work
A manual for outreach practitioners

Jim Sherval, Michelle Rostant, Peggy Dwyer
Centre for HIV/AIDS and Drugs Studies, Lothian Health
Heleen Riper and Dirk Korf
Bonger Institute, University of Amsterdam

Luxembourg: Office for Official publications of the European Communities

2001 — 83 pp. — 20 x 21 cm

ISBN 92-9156-024-3

European Monitoring Centre for Drugs and Drug Addiction
Rua da Cruz de Santa Apolónia 23–25
P-1149–045 Lisboa
Tel. (351) 218 11 30 00
Fax (351) 218 13 17 11
E-mail: info@emcdda.org
http://www.emcdda.org